MAJOR BATTLES OF THE WAR OF 1812

Gordon Clarke

Crabtree Publishing Company

www.crabtreebooks.com

DOCUMENTING THE WAR OF 1812

Author: Gordon Clarke
Editor-in-Chief: Lionel Bender
Editor: Clare Hibbert
**Publishing plan research
and development:**
  Sean Charlebois, Reagan Miller
  Crabtree Publishing Company
Proofreader: Crystal Sikkens
Editorial director: Kathy Middleton
Print coordinator: Katherine Berti
Photo research: Bridget Heos
Designer and Makeup: Ben White
**Production coordinator
  and prepress technician:**
  Margaret Amy Salter
Production: Kim Richardson
Consultant: Richard Jensen,
  Research Professor of History,
  Culver Stockton College, Missouri

  Ronald J. Dale,
  War of 1812 Historian, 1812
  Bicentennial Project Manager,
  Parks Canada
Maps: Stefan Chabluk

Photo credits:
Alamy: 18l (INTERFOTO), 26–27 (North Wind Picture Archives), 28bl (North Wind Picture Archives), 32b (North Wind Picture Archives),
Major-General Sir Isaac Brock, KB [President and Administrator of Upper Canada, 1811-12] by George T. Berthon. 694158. Government of Ontario Art Collection, Archives of Ontario: page 13 (top)
Library of Congress: 1 (LC-USZC4-6294), 4 (pnp/ppmsca.10756), 5 (LC-DIG-ppmsc-05876), 10l (LC-DIG-hec-06811), 10–11 (LC-DIG-pga-02289), 12 (LC-USZC4-509), 12–13 (LC-DIG-ppmsca-23020), 13t (LC-USZ62-121159), 14b (LC-DIG-ppmsca-10753), 15t (LC-DIG-ppmsca-03211), 15b (LC-USZ62-19360), 17 (LC-USZC4-2677), 22–23 (LC-DIG-pga-02823), 23t (LC-USZ61-313), 25 (LC-USZ62-3707), 27t (LC-D416-22695), 28–29 (LC-USZC4-5918), 29r (LC-USZ62-63254), 30t (LC-DIG-ppmsca-23076), 30b (LC-DIG-ppmsca-31112), 32t (LC-USZC2-3030), 35 (LC-DIG-pga-00295), 36b (LC-USZ62-132786) 36–37 (LC-DIG-pga-03275), 37 (LC-DIG-pga-01838), 38 (LC-USZC2-3796),
"The Battle of Queenston Heights" by James B. Dennis, c. 1820-30, courtesy of Riverbrink Art Museum: pages 12–13 (bottom)
shutterstock.com: 3 (Wally Stemberger), 16 (rook76)
Topfoto (The Granger Collection): 9, 18–19, 20, 21, 24, 26, 31, 33, 34, 39, 40, 41
Wikimedia Commons: 1910 painting by Edward Percy Moran. Library of Congress: cover
Cover: A 1910 painting of the Battle of New Orleans by E. Percy Moran, shows Colonel Andrew Jackson standing on his "battlements," with sword raised.
Title page: The U.S.S. *Chesapeake* approaches the H.M.S. *Shannon*

Library and Archives Canada Cataloguing in Publication

Clarke, Gordon, 1965-
  Major battles of the War of 1812 / Gordon Clarke.

(Documenting the War of 1812)
Includes bibliographical references and index.
Issued also in electronic format.
ISBN 978-0-7787-7960-5 (bound).--ISBN 978-0-7787-7965-0 (pbk.)

  1. United States--History--War of 1812--Campaigns--Juvenile literature. 2. Canada--History--War of 1812--Campaigns--Juvenile literature. I. Title. II. Series: Documenting the War of 1812

E355.C53 2011   j973.5'23   C2011-905245-8

Library of Congress Cataloging-in-Publication Data

Clarke, Gordon.
  Major battles of the War of 1812 / by Gordon Clarke.
      p. cm. -- (Documenting the War of 1812)
  Includes bibliographical references and index.
  ISBN 978-0-7787-7960-5 (reinforced library binding : alk. paper) --
ISBN 978-0-7787-7965-0 (pbk. : alk. paper) -- ISBN 978-1-4271-8829-8 (electronic pdf) -- ISBN 978-1-4271-9732-0 (electronic html)
  1. United States--History--War of 1812--Campaigns--Juvenile literature. I. Title. II. Series.

E355.C53 2011
973.5'2--dc23
                                      2011029840

Crabtree Publishing Company

www.crabtreebooks.com   1-800-387-7650

Printed in the U.S.A./102012/CJ20120907

Published in Canada
Crabtree Publishing
616 Welland Ave.
St. Catharines, Ontario
L2M 5V6

Published in the United States
Crabtree Publishing
PMB 59051
350 Fifth Avenue, 59th Floor
New York, New York 10118

Published in the United Kingdom
Crabtree Publishing
Maritime House
Basin Road North, Hove
BN41 1WR

Published in Australia
Crabtree Publishing
3 Charles Street
Coburg North
VIC, 3058

CONTENTS

This book includes images of, and excerpts and
quotes from, documents of the War of 1812. The
documents range from letters, posters, and official
papers to battle plans, paintings, and cartoons.

INTRODUCTION

The American Revolutionary War (1775–1783) ended with the signing of the Treaty of Paris. Less than 30 years later, a combination of factors brought Great Britain and the United States once again to war. The British were unhappy about the loss of their former colonies.

Following their defeat in the Northwest Indian War, many Native North American nations lost their land to questionable land treaties that Americans failed to honor when peace was negotiated. The Shawnee leader Tecumseh began organizing a new confederacy of Native North Americans opposed to

Below: In this 1813 cartoon, the U.S. figure of Columbia (left) lectures John Bull (right), who represents Great Britain, on the subject of free trade. Napoleon Bonaparte (center), whom Columbia nicknames "Beau Napperty," stands between the two.

I tell you Johnny, you must learn to read Respect – Free trade – Seamans rights &c – As for you Mounseer Beau Napperty, when John gets his lesson by heart I'll teach you Respect – Retribution &c. &c.

Ha ha – Begar me be glad to see Madam Columbia angry with dat dere Bull – But me no learn respect – me no learn retribution – Me be de grand Emperor –

I don't like that lesson I'll read this pretty lesson

Above: A caricature shows the wealthy American politician Josiah Quincy (1772–1864), who opposed the War of 1812. The regal coat, scepter, and crown indicate his loyalty to Great Britain.

U.S. Expansionism

In the 1800s, many Americans believed that the United States was destined to expand across the North American continent, from the Atlantic Coast to the Pacific Ocean. They believed that expansion was not only wise but also something they must do for the long-term good of the nation.

U.S. expansion that took away their lands. Conflict between the confederacy and the United States came to a head in the Battle of Tippecanoe (November 7, 1811), when U.S. forces destroyed Tecumseh's village.

Meanwhile, Great Britain was fighting a world war against Napoleonic France, trying to prevent the French conquest of Europe and seizure of colonies around the world. The British fielded the largest navy in the world and used it to blockade European ports to prevent supplies from reaching the French army. To operate this large fleet the British had to impress, or forcibly enlist, sailors to serve in their Navy. The British believed that a person born in their country should remain a subject to the ruler of that country no matter where they moved. British-born sailors who had moved to the United States were forcibly impressed into service from American merchant vessels stopped on the high seas.

Declaration of war

In 1810, about 12 War Hawks were elected to the U.S. Congress. They were called War Hawks because they pushed for war against Great Britain. Their reasons were because of Britain's impressment of U.S. sailors, the refusal to allow U.S. trade with France, and, they believed that Britain supported Native North American uprisings on the western frontier. Great Britain had been at war with France since 1792 and could not spare many soldiers to defend their North American Provinces. The War Hawks thought the war would be over quickly, and that the people of Upper Canada (Ontario) in particular would welcome the U.S. Army as liberators.

A War Between Friends

According to local legend, when the news that war had been declared arrived at Fort George, Canada, the British officers were in the process of hosting their U.S. counterparts from across the Niagara River for dinner. The senior British officer at the dinner insisted that the meal should proceed as normal and that nothing would commence until a later date.

By 1812, the majority of the residents of Upper Canada were recent American immigrants, many of whom had fought against the British in the American Revolution just 30 years before. At the urging of President James Madison, Congress declared war on Great Britain on June 18, 1812.

"The acquisition of Canada this year, as far as the neighborhood of Quebec, will be a mere matter of marching."

Thomas Jefferson, August 1812

Below: A map of North America shows country, state, and territory boundaries at the start of the War of 1812.

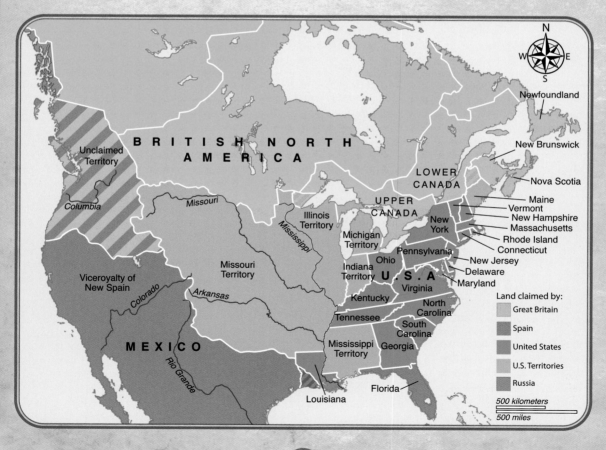

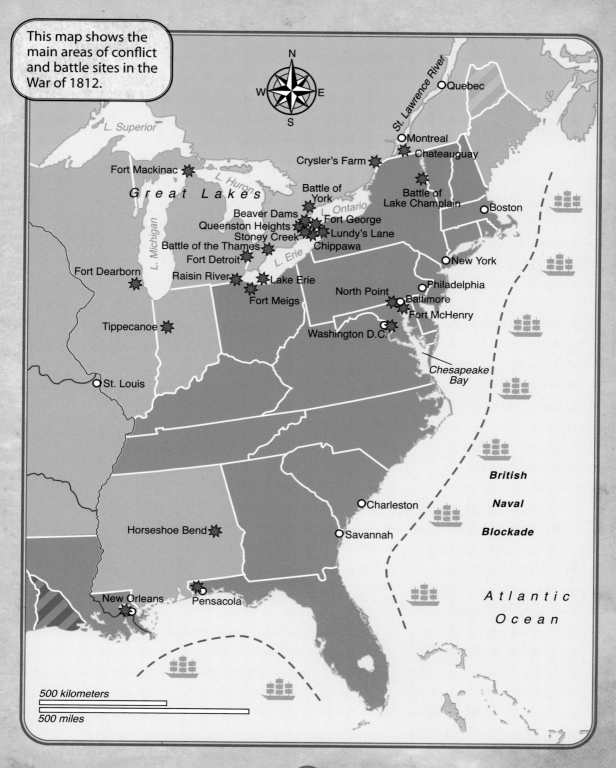

This map shows the main areas of conflict and battle sites in the War of 1812.

N
W E
S

L. Superior

Quebec

St. Lawrence River

Montreal

Fort Mackinac

Crysler's Farm

Chateauguay

L. Huron

Great Lakes

L. Ontario

Battle of York

Battle of Lake Champlain

Beaver Dams

Boston

Queenston Heights

Fort George

L. Michigan

Stoney Creek

Lundy's Lane

Battle of the Thames

Chippawa

L. Erie

New York

Fort Dearborn

Fort Detroit

Raisin River

Lake Erie

Philadelphia

Fort Meigs

North Point

Baltimore

Tippecanoe

Fort McHenry

Washington D.C.

St. Louis

Chesapeake Bay

Charleston

Horseshoe Bend

Savannah

British

Naval

Blockade

New Orleans

Pensacola

Atlantic Ocean

500 kilometers

500 miles

Chapter One: The War in the Great Lakes

The Capture of Fort Mackinac

As soon as war was declared, the British sent word to their troops westward by canoe courier. The Americans sent messages by mail. The courier was faster, and this gave the British an advantage. They were able to capture the westernmost U.S. position, Fort Mackinac, before its commander even knew that war had been declared.

Brock and Tecumseh Meet

The most important British commander was General Isaac Brock and his ally was Shawnee War Chief, Tecumseh. Brock said of Tecumseh, "a more . . . gallant warrior does not, I believe, exist." Tecumseh, returning to his followers after meeting Brock said, "This is a man!"

The United States put little effort into developing supply lines, building ships, or training soldiers because they expected that war would be over swiftly, especially with Canadians supporting the American side. The U.S. plan was to invade Canada in four locations in quick succession: Amherstburg (near Detroit), Niagara, Kingston, and Montreal.

The Detroit Frontier

The first invasion by U.S. soldiers into Canada was led by General William Hull, who brought his troops across the Detroit River into Canada at the town of Sandwich in July 1812. However, while waiting for new supplies he received word that Fort Mackinac had already fallen to the British. Hull retreated back across the river to Fort Detroit.

The Fort Dearborn Massacre

Anticipating that Fort Dearborn on the Chicago River would be the next target, Hull sent orders that its commander, Captain Nathan Heald, evacuate. Heald negotiated with nearby Pottawatomi Natives and agreed to turn over the fort and its contents if they would allow the Americans to retreat in peace. Heald broke the agreement and destroyed the fort's supplies. Pottawatomi warriors attacked the retreating Americans. Fifty-two Americans were killed and 41 taken prisoner.

The surrender of Detroit

Hull worried that Fort Detroit would be the next to fall and that his own troops would be massacred.

The British commander in Upper Canada, General Isaac Brock, arrived in the area along with the Shawnee, led by Tecumseh and other Native North American nations. Brock and Tecumseh managed to make the Americans believe that they were greatly outnumbered when, in fact, they were not. Hull surrendered to General Brock on August 16, 1812.

The surrender of Fort Detroit left most of the U.S. Northwest Territory undefended. The victory strengthened Tecumseh's influence in the Native North American community, cemented their support against the Americans in the area, and encouraged new Native attacks on U.S. outposts. Meanwhile, Brock returned to Fort George in Niagara.

Above: This 19th-century engraving shows U.S. General William Hull arriving at his decision to surrender Fort Detroit to the British on August 16, 1812.

Above: An engraving shows Commodore Oliver Hazard Perry, who led U.S. naval forces to victory at the Battle of Lake Erie.

The River Raisin Massacre

Following a defeat at Frenchtown, Michigan, many U.S. soldiers were taken prisoner. Most were Kentuckians. As they were being moved to Detroit in January 1813, the wounded prisoners left behind were massacred by Native warriors at the River Raisin. From 30 to 100 were killed.

The Battle of Lake Erie

In the spring of 1813, Commodore Oliver Hazard Perry was given command of the U.S. fleet on Lake Erie. He immediately set out to build up naval forces on the lake. By late summer, Perry was ready to challenge the British fleet at Amherstburg. British supplies to Fort Amherstburg and Detroit were threatened and British Commodore Robert Barclay attacked Perry's squadron on September 10, 1813. Perry's flagship, the U.S.S. *Lawrence*, was almost completely destroyed during battle. He rallied the remaining American ships and attacked the British. Unable to withstand this second wave of attacks, the British surrendered. Perry's victory marked a turning point in the war on the Detroit frontier. The British had lost control of Lake Erie and could no longer supply their forces, including their Native allies. They evacuated Detroit and abandoned Fort Malden. Perry reported the victory to General William Henry Harrison:

> *We have met the enemy and they are ours. Two ships, two brigs, one schooner, and one sloop. Yours with great respect and esteem,*

The Battle of the Thames

The command of the U.S. Army of the Northwest passed to William Henry Harrison. He wanted to destroy the retreating British army and their Native allies. This would prevent them from reinforcing the British at Niagara and retaking Fort George. Harrison's army reoccupied Detroit while pursuing the British army now under Brock's replacement,

Above: Produced 65 years after the event, this print shows the U.S. and British navies meeting on Lake Erie on the United States–Canada border.

"Remember the Raisin!"

Memory of the River Raisin Massacre became a battle cry, used to rally American troops at the Battle of the Thames. It was also used to recruit soldiers in Kentucky.

Major-General Henry Procter. The British and Native allies made a stand at the Thames River near what is now Chatham, Ontario. Harrison's army quickly defeated the British on October 5, 1813. Tecumseh and other Native warriors continued to fight until they too were overwhelmed by the much larger American force. Tecumseh was killed in the battle. Without his leadership, the Native North American confederacy soon fell apart, and some Nations' chiefs informed Harrison that they were quitting the war.

Below: This hand-colored print shows the death of Tecumseh at the Battle of the Thames on October 5, 1813. He was shot by Colonel Richard M. Johnson, who was leading the Kentucky mounted volunteers.

The Niagara Frontier

The Niagara Frontier saw the first significant battle of the war. In September 1812, Stephen Van Rensselaer received orders from the Secretary of War that he should proceed with his planned attack.

The Battle of Queenston Heights
The Americans crossed the Niagara River before dawn on October 13, while the British fired at their boats. However, the Americans landed more than 800 soldiers that overwhelmed the 300 British defenders of Queenston. General Isaac Brock arrived from Fort George and rallied the troops to retake a

British cannon battery that had been overrun by the Americans but was killed while leading the charge. Other British officers were hit, and the British retreated into the village of Queenston.

British reinforcements from Fort George began to arrive at Queenston Heights at the same time as about 100 Six Nations warriors, led by Mohawk chief John Norton. Together they attacked the American positions. British troops, Canadian militiamen, and warriors skirmished with the Americans and prevented them from preparing proper defenses. General Van Rensselaer crossed back to Lewiston to get more men and arrange the next attack, but most American militiamen lost their nerve when they heard the fierce war cries of the warriors, saw the wounded returning from battle, and overestimated the number of British reinforcements marching from Fort George.

Below: This oil painting depicts the American advance across the Niagara River in the Battle of Queenston Heights.

Below: The much-admired General Brock bolstered the spirits of troops and civilians. He wrote, "Most of the people have lost all confidence—I however speak loud and look big."

The British, now led by Major-General Roger Hale Sheaffe, led a charge that forced the Americans back to the edge of the escarpment. Many Americans fell to their deaths racing down the escarpment or drowned in the swift waters of the Niagara while trying to swim to safety. With no reinforcements or means of escape they were forced to surrender. The British won the battle, but lost their best military leader, Isaac Brock.

Armstrong and the Great Lakes

Late in 1812, Captain Isaac Chauncey took command of U.S. naval forces on lakes Erie and Ontario. He built up his fleet ready for an attack in the spring. In February 1813, John Armstrong, the new U.S. Secretary of War, ordered Chauncey and Major-General Henry Dearborn to cooperate in a campaign to capture Kingston and Niagara, and to destroy the shipyard at York (now Toronto).

Below: In this cartoon from 1814, King George III shovels new ships into a bread oven. The image makes fun of the desperate attempts by the British to recover after their naval losses on the Great Lakes in 1813 and 1814.

Patent Oven for Bakeing Ships

French Dough Trough

The Battle of York

In April 1813, Chauncey's fleet sailed for York, carrying 1,700 of Dearborn's troops. The first wave of U.S. soldiers landed west of York and advanced on the town, supported by fire from Chauncey's ships. The outnumbered British took heavy losses and retreated to Fort York. British Major-General Roger Hale Scheaffe ordered a further retreat toward Kingston. He also commanded an officer to destroy the main magazine at Fort York so that it would not fall into U.S. hands. The magazine exploded and killed or wounded about 250 U.S. soldiers. For the next three days, U.S. soldiers looted empty houses in York and set fire to the town's legislative buildings.

Above: U.S. General Zebulon Pike was killed by flying debris at the Battle of York, after the British blew up their ammunition stores.

The Battle of Fort George

Following their victory at the Battle of York, the U.S. troops moved to Fort Niagara to prepare for an assault on Fort George, directly across the Niagara River. Beginning on May 25, 1813, the Americans began to bombard Fort George. Landing on the shore of Lake Ontario on May 27 rather than the river, 5,000 Americans were opposed by several hundred, British, Canadians, and Native allies. The U.S. soldiers, with help from U.S. naval forces, inflicted heavy casualties on the British. As the third wave was landing, the British commanding officer realized he would soon be surrounded and ordered a retreat of his remaining soldiers to Queenston and finally to Burlington Heights (now Hamilton, Ontario).

The Battle of Stoney Creek

Following the Battle of Fort George, the Americans sent an army to capture the British Army at Burlington Heights. The Americans' much larger army set up camp at Stoney Creek and planned to attack the next day. British General John Vincent led a surprise attack in the middle of the night. Two U.S. generals were captured, and the remaining Americans retreated toward the town of Niagara. This marked the farthest point of the U.S. advance from Niagara.

The Battle of Beaver Dams

Three weeks later, U.S. soldiers set out from Fort George with the intention of taking a lightly manned British post at Beaver Dams. Laura Secord, the wife of a local militia sergeant, overheard the U.S. officers discussing the possibility of an attack. She set out to warn the British forces, walking about 12 miles (19 kilometers) through the woods. She ran across a Native encampment and the warriors took her to Lieutenant James Fitzgibbon, who commanded the British outpost. Her warning allowed Fitzgibbon to set an ambush for the advancing U.S. troops on June 22. When the Americans attacked on June 24, 1813, they were ambushed by Fitzgibbon's Native allies. After being wounded in the battle that followed, the U.S. commander, Colonel Charles Boerstler, surrendered.

Recapture of Fort Niagara

As 1813 wore on, the Americans prepared for an attack on Montreal. Most of the soldiers who had been in the Niagara area were moved to Sackets Harbor on the other side of Lake Ontario. The U.S. commander, Brigadier-General George McClure, felt that Fort George could no longer be defended as he was now outnumbered by the British, so he ordered his troops across the river to Fort Niagara. The U.S. troops evacuated on December 10, 1813. As they retreated, the troops set fire to the Canadian town of Niagara (now Niagara-on-the-Lake), leaving many of the inhabitants without shelter as winter began.

Below: This Canadian stamp commemorates Laura Secord, whose bravery contributed to a British victory at the Battle of Beaver Dams on June 24, 1813.

LAURA SECORD *LEGENDARY PATRIOT*
HÉROÏNE LÉGENDAIRE

CANADA 42

The War in the American West

Fort Madison had been built along the Mississippi River in 1808 in order to assert U.S. land claims, following an 1804 treaty with the Sauk. The Sauk war chief Black Hawk argued the legality of the 1804 treaty, however, and led several attacks on the fort. By July 1813, any movement outside Fort Madison was impossible. It was abandoned in September.

Along with other warriors from various Native nations, the Sauk warriors continued efforts to fight U.S. expansion into the western territories. By September 1814, Black Hawk's warriors had forced U.S. troops out of most of the upper Mississippi River valley. At the end of the war the western territories were returned to the United States, but fighting continued for several years between the Americans and the Native Americans in the area, including the Sauk.

Nine days later, the British forces, led by Lieutenant Colonel Murray, crossed the river and stormed their way into Fort Niagara. They then set fire to the U.S. towns of Lewiston and Buffalo, in retaliation for the Americans' burning Niagara.

In the campaigns of 1812 and 1813, the U.S. Army won only when they greatly outnumbered their enemy. The U.S. Army established camps of instruction to raise the skill level of troops to match that of the British regulars and Canadian militia they were facing. Both sides felt that the French would soon be defeated in Europe and that would free up a very large and professional British force to fight in North America. The year 1814 would be the last good opportunity for the Americans to capture Upper Canada.

Above: This print of Black Hawk was produced in the 1830s for a history of North American Natives.

Fighting Talk

"Let me lay my sword against his." Colonel Charles Boerstler hoped to defeat Fitzgibbon personally, but the British commander was the victor.

The Battle of Lundy's Lane

U.S. Major-General Jacob Brown wanted to attack Kingston, but Chauncey would not supply ships for the campaign. Instead, Brown moved his troops to Buffalo and recaptured Fort Erie. He hoped to advance as far as Burlington Heights, which is present-day Hamilton.

On July 5, 1814, Brown's army advanced toward Niagara but was met by a smaller British force at Chippawa, south of Niagara Falls. In a bloody battle, the British were driven back by the well-trained Americans. This was the first time in history that an American army beat a roughly equal force of regulars on the open field. The British retreated back to Fort George and Brown's army followed.

Chauncey's fleet failed to arrive to help with an attack on Fort George, Fort Niagara, and Fort Mississauga. Instead, he retreated toward Chippawa. The British followed, positioning themselves at Lundy's Lane where it crossed the road to Burlington. Brown decided to march his troops from Chippawa to drive the British from this key position.

On July 25, General Gordon Drummond had arrived at Fort George.

Left: An officer's saber, shown here, is similar to one's used in the U.S. Army during the first few decades of the 1800s. The weapon's curved, single-edged blade was deadly in one-to-one combat.

He ordered troops from Burlington and Fort George to reinforce the position at Lundy's Lane. The first Brigade of the U.S. Army, led by Brigadier-General Winfield Scott, arrived at Lundy's Lane (present-day Niagara Falls, Ontario) shortly after Drummond's men.

A major battle began around 6 p.m. Neither side gained a clear advantage. By midnight, both sides were exhausted. Major-General Jacob Brown who arrived to support Scott's troops feared that U.S. supplies of water and ammunition would run out and ordered a retreat to Fort Erie.

The Battle of Lundy's Lane was one of the bloodiest battles of the war. Each side had more than 850 men dead or wounded. The losses meant that Brown was left with too few men to continue toward Burlington Heights.

Below: The Battle of Lundy's Lane, depicted in this 19th-century watercolor, was a bloody affair.

The Siege of Fort Erie

Brown's men built up the defenses of
Fort Erie as Drummond moved slowly
to recover the territory. Drummond
attempted to retake Fort Erie, but failed
to do so. After almost two months of
fighting, he ordered his troops to return
to Fort George. Fearing that he would
not be able to get supplies through the
winter, Brown abandoned Fort Erie.
He burned it to the ground and moved
his troops to Sackets Harbor.

Below: The British besieged
U.S troops at Fort Erie during
August and September 1814. This
contemporary map shows the
site of the fort, and its defenses.

The St. Lawrence Campaign

Part of Secretary Armstrong's plan to win the war was to take Montreal. If they succeeded, it would cut off British supply lines in Upper Canada. The U.S. plan called for two separate advances, one toward Kingston led by Major-General James Wilkinson, and the other toward Montreal led by Major-General Wade Hampton.

The Battle of the Chateauguay

Hampton began to move more than 4,000 men toward Montreal in late September 1813, arriving at the Chateauguay River, which flows into the St. Lawrence near Montreal. Lieutenant Colonel Charles de Salaberry, who commanded the outposts around Montreal, had his 1,530 Canadian regulars, militia, and Mohawk warriors prepare defenses along the Chateauguay River.

Hampton split his men and attempted to cross the Chateauguay in two locations, but both groups found themselves pinned down by de Salaberry's forward defenses. Hampton then became aware of the reserve groups beyond the front. Fearing that he was outnumbered, he commanded his men to retreat. Hampton decided that another attack on Montreal would not succeed, and returned to winter quarters in New York State.

Right: A line engraving shows the Canadian commander Charles de Salaberry, who successfully held off the U.S. advance at the Chateauguay River in October 1813.

The Battle of Crysler's Farm

On November 10, a portion of Major-General James Wilkinson's army of about 8,000 men that was set on the capture of Montreal, camped on one side of John Crysler's farm, near present-day Cornwall, Ontario. Just up river on the other side of the farm was a small British force under Lieutenant Colonel Joseph Morrison. On November 11, the American force of some 2,500 men under Brigadier-General John Boyd attacked the British position. Boyd's men were defeated and forced to retreat to Cornwall.

Wilkinson learned of Hampton's loss at Chateauguay and decided to follow Hampton back across the St. Lawrence to New York State for the winter. The defeats at Chateauguay and Crysler's Farm caused the Americans to abandon thoughts of capturing Montreal and prevented the United States from taking over Upper Canada (Ontario).

The Battle of Lake Champlain

Following the defeat of Napoleonic France in 1814, the British were tired of war. From the beginning of the War of 1812 they attempted to get the Americans to negotiate an end to the war. Now thousands of British troops and hundreds of ships were freed up to finally force Americans to discuss an end to the war. Lieutenant-General George Prevost was ordered to take control of Lake Champlain and capture the American town of Plattsburgh to threaten a further advance toward New York City. He advanced to a position outside of Plattsburgh, New York, and waited for the arrival of H.M.S. *Confiance*, which would be the largest ship on Lake Champlain, and the rest of the small British fleet. Brigadier-General Alexander Macomb commanded the U.S.

To the Victor

Following Macdonough's victory at the Battle of Lake Champlain, the British naval officers offered him their swords. Macdonough replied, "Gentlemen, return your swords into your scabbards and wear them. You are worthy of them." This was unusual, but shows the respect that the adversaries had for one another.

Below: An 1816 engraving shows Macdonough's victory at the Battle of Lake Champlain, also known as the Battle of Plattsburgh, on September 11, 1814.

troops at Plattsburgh, along with a naval detachment under the command of Master Commandant Thomas Macdonough, who positioned his ships for the coming attack.

When H.M.S. *Confiance* arrived, it engaged the U.S. fleet right away, and both sides suffered significant damage. Then Macdonough used his anchors to wind around his flagship, the U.S.S. *Saratoga*, so that a fresh side was facing the British fleet. The barrage that followed forced two British ships to surrender. The rest of the fleet retreated back up the lake. Prevost, seeing the naval battle had been lost, ordered his troops to retreat back to Canada. This was a major victory for the U.S. Navy. They had successfully prevented the largest British invasion force of the war from capturing and holding the southern end of Lake Champlain. This victory was one reason why the United States–Canadian border remained unchanged at the negotiations of the Treaty of Ghent, as neither side had gained any significant ground.

Below: Taken from an original portrait by John Wesley Jarvis, this engraving shows U.S. Commodore Thomas Macdonough in his naval uniform.

Chapter Two: The Atlantic Theater of the War

At the outset of the war, the British believed that the Americans would be no match for the powerful Royal Navy. There were more than 600 British warships on the oceans, but only a small number were available for the defense of British North America. The fledgling U.S. Navy had fewer ships, but they were more powerful. U.S. commanders knew that their ships were outnumbered, but nevertheless believed that they could do well in one-on-one battles.

The large British Navy had trouble finding enough sailors for its ships and often forced sailors aboard through impressment. By contrast, U.S. sailors were all volunteers and eager to defend their

Below: This brig's plans were drawn in 1845—however, the design of its wooden hull is unchanged from those boats built for the War of 1812.

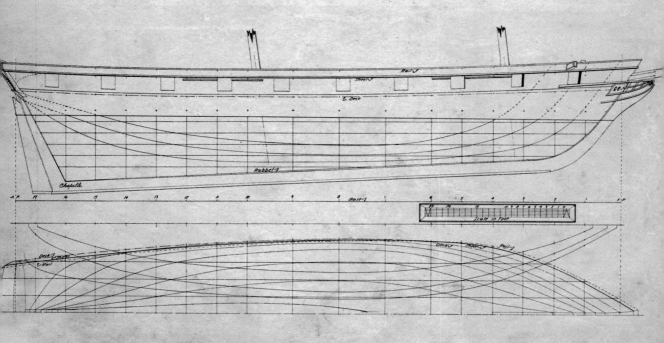

new country. They had better living conditions and were better paid than their British counterparts, and officers could pick and choose from the best trained applicants because there were so few American ships requiring crews.

Licensed to attack

The U.S. Navy increased their naval forces by privateering, which means to outfit private merchant ships for war. Privateers could weaken an enemy's economy by interfering with trade. Both U.S. and British governments harnessed the skills and resources of the large number of privately owned merchant ships. These ships were issued letters of marque—simply put, such letters were a government license to attack and capture enemy ships. The captured ship and its cargo were then sold and the profits divided up amongst the privateers, owners, and crew.

Successful privateers, such as Nova Scotian Joseph Barss and American Thomas Boyle, captured more than 50 opponents' vessels each.

Below: Built for privateering, the U.S. brig *General Armstrong* is seen here firing on British boats at the Battle of Fayal in September 1814.

The American Patriotic Song-Book sheet music:

THE
AMERICAN
PATRIOTIC SONG-BOOK

HUZZA, FOR THE AMERICAN TARS;
OR, HULL AND VICTORY.

WRITTEN BY CHARLES HARFORD.

On the capture of the Guerrierre, a British Frigate, of 49 guns, by Captain Hull, of the American Frigate Constitution, of 44 guns, after an action of 30 minutes, when the Guerriere was blown up.

Ye brave defenders of your country's

cause, Receive the triumph of its loud ap-

flight, Who dar'd our tars to meet him in the

fight : Three cheers proclaim'd the Constitution

tree From vaunting threats of ruthless tyranny.

Allegretto.

Columbia's banners now proclaim her tars Tri-

Second Time Chorus.

umphant ride the sea ; And glo - ry swells the

U.S.S. *Constitution* **captures H.M.S.** *Guerriere*
The war's first major naval confrontation happened on August 19, 1812, when H.M.S. *Guerriere* left a British convoy on the way to Halifax to challenge the much larger U.S.S. *Constitution*.

The *Constitution* was a sturdy frigate with more and larger cannons, and many more crew than the *Guerriere*. One of *Guerriere*'s initial shots simply bounced off *Constitution*'s hull. This is where the *Constitution* got its nickname, "Old Ironsides." When the two ships came within 75 feet (23 meters) of each other, *Constitution*'s captain, Isaac Hull, gave the order to open fire: "Now boys, pour it into them!" The larger U.S. crew was able to fire more and heavier guns than the British and soon the *Guerriere* was so badly damaged that it was no longer seaworthy. The defeat of a major warship was a surprise to the British, but they saw it as a one-off and did not expect it to happen again.

Above: Printed sheet music from *The American Patriotic Song-Book* (1813) was published to celebrate the victory of U.S.S. *Constitution* over H.M.S. *Guerriere*.

Yet, for the remainder of 1812, fast U.S. ships, such as the U.S.S. *Hornet* and the U.S.S. *Wasp*, continued to harass British ships in one-on-one confrontations. In October, the U.S.S. *United States*, under Captain Stephen Decatur, captured H.M.S. *Macedonian* in the mid-Atlantic. In December 1812, the U.S.S. *Constitution* sunk H.M.S. *Java*.

A British blockade

With the loss of three major ships, the British finally recognized that the U.S. Navy frigates were larger than their British counterparts and their crews were better trained. British Admiral Sir John Warren sent more ships and began a blockade of U.S. ports. He also ensured that Royal Navy ships no longer sailed alone.

Royal Navy ships patrolled the East Coast of the United States to prevent trade with Europe and to

Below: The U.S. sloop-of-war *Wasp*'s capture of the British brig *Frolic* is the subject of this 20th-century painting by William Steeple Davis. *Wasp* took on a British convoy under the protection of *Frolic* on October 18, 1812.

Below: In this 19th-century painting, the crew of the victorious frigate *Constitution* fire on the badly damaged H.M.S. *Guerriere*.

Below: In this 1813 cartoon by George Cruikshank, a boarding party from the *Shannon* overwhelms the *Chesapeake*'s crew and hoists the British flag.

Down with your Colours you Smabs down with your Stripes or D— me we'll Stripe you

Above: British ships blockade Chesapeake Bay at the outset of the War of 1812.

hinder resupply up the coast. This forced U.S. merchants to use more expensive overland routes for the transportation of their goods. U.S. naval ships were now confined to the safety of their ports. There were so few ships in the U.S. Navy that it was not worth the risk of trying to run the blockade.

H.M.S. *Shannon* captures U.S.S. *Chesapeake*
On June 1, 1813, Captain James Lawrence brought the U.S.S. *Chesapeake* out of Boston Harbor with a fresh crew to battle H.M.S. *Shannon*. Lawrence was severely injured during the exchange of fire and later died of his wounds. The *Shannon*'s sailors boarded and captured the *Chesapeake*. During the battle more than 80 sailors were killed. The victory restored the confidence of the British Navy.

"Don't give up the ship!" was one of the final commands from Captain James Lawrence after he was mortally wounded aboard the *Chesapeake*. These words were later sewn on to the battle flag of the U.S.S. *Lawrence*.

The Chesapeake Campaign

Canada's governor-general, Sir George Prevost, asked Vice Admiral Sir Alexander Cochrane to retaliate for some of the destruction done by U.S. soldiers in Upper Canada. Cochrane and Major-General Robert Ross decided to attack Washington, D.C., which was not as well defended as the larger industrial town of Baltimore. On August 24, 1814, the British entered Washington with little resistance.

Above: A view of the White House in Washington, D.C. The president's house was set on fire in 1814 by advancing British troops to encourage the Americans to negotiate with Great Britain to bring an end to the war.

President Madison managed to escape just ahead of the oncoming British. His wife, Dolley, left the White House only minutes ahead of its capture. Ross's soldiers set fire to various government buildings, including the White House, the Treasury, and the House of Representatives.

The following day a major storm brought heavy rains that put out the fires as the British returned to their ships. Cochrane and Ross set sail for their next target, the major economic center and port of Baltimore, Maryland.

Above: This drawing by George Munger records the fire-damage done to the U.S. Capitol by the British in 1814.

Below: In this contemporary cartoon, President Madison and his Secretary of War flee Washington as it burns, clutching bundles of papers.

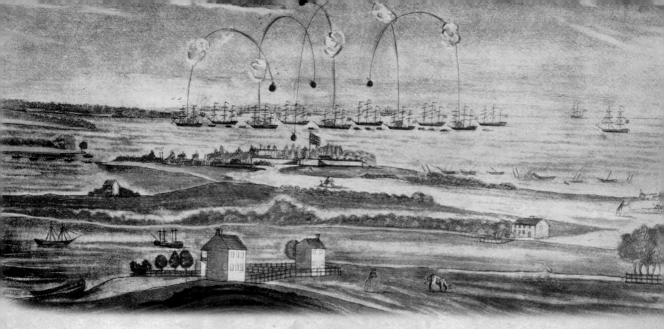

The bombardment of Fort McHenry

Anticipating an attack on Baltimore, Major-General Samuel Smith of the Maryland Militia had built many defenses around the city. Ross and Cochrane planned a land attack on Baltimore under cover of cannon fire from the Royal Navy. They landed more than 4,000 soldiers 12 miles (20 km) along the coast. The soldiers were met by 3,200 members of the Maryland Militia under Brigadier-General John Stricker, who had set his men in a favorable position. In the ensuing Battle of North Point the Americans were routed while the British lost General Ross, killed by an American rifleman. They were not able to exploit this victory, however, because Fort McHenry could not be neutralized.

Early on September 13, 1814, the British fleet began to shell Baltimore's Fort McHenry. It did so from the maximum range of its artillery, as the British approach was blocked by a line of 22 merchant ships that had been intentionally sunk in the harbor. While the bombardment was happening, Stricker's men held their position and killed Major-General Ross. Ross was replaced by Colonel Arthur Brooke. The naval bombardment continued for 25 hours, but had limited effect.

Above: British ships in Baltimore Harbor fruitlessly bombard Fort McHenry during September 13 and 14, 1814.

The star-spangled banner

Early the following morning, the commander of Fort McHenry, Major George Armistead, raised a huge U.S. flag—32 x 42 feet (10 x 13 meters)—which had been sewn by local flag maker Mary Pickersgill. McHenry's visual sign that the fort had withstood the bombardment inspired a local lawyer, Francis Scott Key, to write a poem called "The Star-Spangled Banner," which became the U.S. national anthem. Seeing that the fort was still in U.S. hands, Brooke abandoned his attack, took his troops back to their ships, and set sail for the south. The successful defense of Baltimore served to rally American morale following the burning of Washington.

Left: The U.S. flag became known as the Star-Spangled Banner during the War of 1812. Here, the figure of Columbia raises the flag.

Below: Shown here is the manuscript of the first stanza of "The Star-Spangled Banner," written by Baltimore lawyer Francis Scott Key in 1814.

The Star-spangled banner.

O say! can you see by the dawn's early light
What so proudly we hail'd at the twilight's last gleaming
Whose broad stripes and bright stars, through the clouds of the fight,
O'er the ramparts we watch'd were so gallantly streaming?
And the rocket's red glare - the bomb bursting in air
Gave proof through the night that our flag was still there!
O say, does that star-spangled banner yet wave
O'er the land of the free & the home of the brave? —

Chapter Three: Battles of the Southern Theater

The War of 1812 reached the southmost parts of the United States. There, U.S. forces destroyed the Creek nation and defeated its invasion force at New Orleans on the Gulf Coast.

The Creek War

In the southeastern United States, the Native Creek nation became divided over whether to continue their recent path of assimilation with white settlers or join Tecumseh's confederacy against U.S. expansionism. The Creek were divided on the issue and it created a civil war within their nation.

Below: After the American Revolution, large areas of the continent remained colonies, but the United States slowly worked to expand its borders. This oil painting of New Orleans celebrates President Jefferson's Louisiana Purchase of 1803.

UNDER MY WINGS EVERY THING PROSPERS

The White Sticks, led by the older Creek chiefs, favored friendship with the settlers. The other, smaller group, the Red Sticks, fought U.S. expansion.

On July 27, 1813, a confrontation took place between the Red Sticks and a group of U.S. soldiers from Fort Mims, Alabama. Known as the Battle of Burnt Corn, it was considered a declaration of war. Red Stick leaders Peter McQueen and William Weatherhead led an attack on Fort Mims on August 30, 1813. About 250 U.S. soldiers suffered terrible deaths. Many Creek warriors died, too. Most Creeks wished to remain on good terms with the United States, but very few Americans made the distinction between the Red Sticks and the White Sticks.

A militia force, led by Colonel Andrew Jackson, was formed to fight the Red Sticks. On March 27, 1814, Jackson's force of 2,700 West Tennessee militia and regular U.S. infantry and about 600 Choctaw, Cherokee, and White Sticks launched an attack on the Red Stick camp at Horseshoe Bend in central

Below: In this 1843 engraving, Chief William Weatherford, leader of the Red Sticks, surrenders to Colonel Andrew Jackson. The Red Sticks were defeated at the Battle of Horseshoe Bend on March 27, 1814.

Alabama. The battle was a victory for Jackson. Most of the 1,000 Red Sticks warriors were killed in battle or massacred afterward—just 200 escaped to Florida. In August 1814, Jackson forced the remaining Creeks, who had fought beside him at Horseshoe Bend, to sign the Treaty of Fort Jackson, turning over 23 million acres (93,000 square kilometers) of Creek land to the U.S. government.

The American South

Great Britain devoted a larger number of troops and ships to the war in North America following its victory in the war against Napoleon. The British planned to attack the southern United States and secure the mouth of the Mississippi River, cutting off a major U.S. commerce route. They set up a base at Pensacola, Florida, in August 1814 to prepare. The Americans anticipated the attack and ordered Andrew Jackson to New Orleans to take charge of the city's defenses. The British were attempting to force the Americans to negotiate an end to the war and this would give them a strong bargaining chip.

Above: Colonel Andrew Jackson is shown here on horseback in 1814, leading his Tennessee forces. Jackson later served as the seventh president of the United States.

The Battle of New Orleans
In December 1814, a British fleet under Vice Admiral Sir Alexander Cochrane arrived in the Gulf of Mexico near New Orleans. The British spent three days attempting to round up a hastily assembled collection of seven U.S. ships, eventually capturing them on December 14 in Lake Borgne. Next, the British began moving thousands of troops ashore to prepare for the attack. Although the United States had lost the naval confrontation, the three days bought Jackson valuable time for building up defenses and gathering men around New Orleans.

Approximately 1,800 British troops reached the Mississippi River on December 23 and set up camp for the night. Jackson sent men to attack the British as they slept, and inflicted a nasty blow. Both sides retreated to get ready for the next round of fighting.

Jackson took up a position at the Chalmette Plantation along the Rodriguez Canal. His collection of about 6,000 men included regular army units, the New Orleans militia, former slaves, Kentucky and Tennessee frontiersmen, and Jean Lafitte's pirates. Jackson had his men build a large wall of logs, mud, and cotton bales between the Mississippi River and a huge cypress swamp. Behind these "ramparts," the men set up every piece of artillery they could get their hands on.

General Edward Pakenham took command of the British troops on Christmas Day and launched an assault three days later. The two sides exchanged cannon fire but Pakenham called off the assault as his supplies ran low.

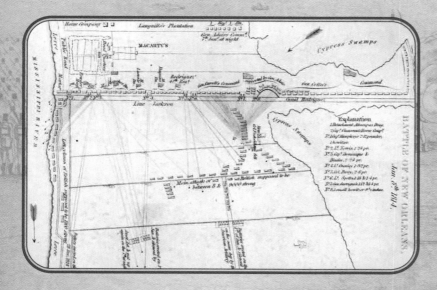

Above: A map showing troop positions in the Battle of New Orleans, January 8, 1815.

Reinforcements arrived and Pakenham now had 8,000 men at his disposal. He planned a two-pronged assault on the U.S. position and launched his attack early in the morning of January 8. The British advance was meant to take place under the cover of the morning fog, but their passage through the swamp was slow. By the time the British emerged for the attack, the fog had lifted and they became easy targets for the American riflemen.

General Pakenham and his second-in-command, General Gibbs, were both killed early in the battle. With no one to order them to advance or retreat, the British soldiers were mowed down in the open area in front of Jackson's ramparts. Eventually, the British sounded a retreat and returned to their ships. Jackson had successfully defended New Orleans despite being slightly outnumbered.

Below: Jackson commands his troops at the Battle of New Orleans. Thanks to his defensive strategies, the United States was able to hold New Orleans.

The Battle of Fort Bowyer

With the attack on New Orleans unsuccessful, the British made plans to move on to their next target, Mobile, Alabama. The first step in that campaign was to capture Fort Bowyer, in Mobile Bay.

The British had already tried and failed to capture Fort Bowyer by attacking the front off the Gulf of Mexico the previous September. This time, British General John Lambert landed 1,400 men away from the fort and had them come around from the rear. The British set up artillery and bombarded the fort for five days. Then, on February 11, 1815, Major William Lawrence surrendered.

Having secured Mobile Bay, the British prepared to move on Mobile. Two days after the capture of Fort Bowyer, however, H.M.S. *Brazen* arrived with word that the war was over. The attack on Mobile was called off, and the British fleet sailed for its base in the West Indies.

Below: In this 19th-century painting of the Battle of New Orleans by E. Percy Moran, Colonel Andrew Jackson stands on his "battlements," with his sword raised.

Chapter Four: The End of the War of 1812

Talks to end the war began in July 1814 in the Belgian city of Ghent. The negotiating teams from both sides were given unrealistic instructions from their governments. The U.S. delegation was told to demand that Upper and Lower Canada be given to the United States. The British delegation, expecting large numbers of British troops from Europe to arrive in Canada shortly, was told to negotiate to keep the part of Maine that interfered with the route from New Brunswick and Quebec and to return southwestern Upper Canada to Canadian control. They also wanted a territory established for Native peoples west of the Mississippi River as outlined in the Treaty of Grenville of 1795.

The official end

Negotiations went nowhere for several months until other pressures made both sides work harder to find an agreement.

Below: Shown here is the title page of the report of the Hartford Convention, at which representatives from New England met to discuss possible succession from the United States.

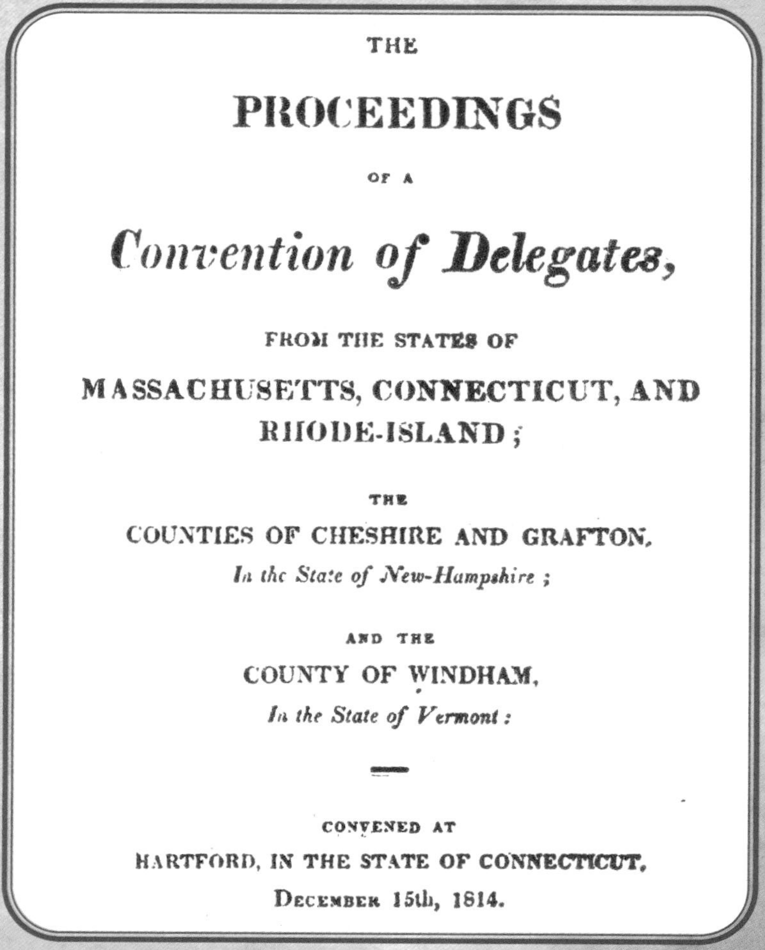

THE

PROCEEDINGS

OF A

Convention of Delegates,

FROM THE STATES OF

MASSACHUSETTS, CONNECTICUT, AND RHODE-ISLAND;

THE

COUNTIES OF CHESHIRE AND GRAFTON.
In the State of New-Hampshire;

AND THE

COUNTY OF WINDHAM,
In the State of Vermont:

CONVENED AT

HARTFORD, IN THE STATE OF CONNECTICUT,
DECEMBER 15th, 1814.

The British began to worry that war could restart in Europe. The U.S. economy was crumbling, and there was talk of the New England states separating to form their own confederation.

By mid-November, both sides looked to put the war behind them, and agreed that the United States–Canada border should go back to where it was before the war. The final details took time to work out but the peace treaty was agreed to on December 24, 1814. Interestingly, none of the reasons for declaring war in the first place were addressed by the treaty. The official end to the war came on February 16, 1815, following the ratification of the Treaty of Ghent by the United States.

Fighting continued for several weeks following ratification, as word of the treaty took time to reach the various ships and frontiers from the negotiating teams in Belgium.

Above: This oil on canvas by Forestier captures the moment on December 24, 1814, when British and U.S. diplomats signed the Treaty of Ghent in Belgium.

Winners and losers

The War of 1812 is often referred to as "the war both sides won." Certainly, Americans and Canadians have both claimed it as a victory since then. The Canadians successfully repelled several invasions of their land, while the Americans considered it a successful "second War of Independence." The Native people, on the other hand, could not claim victory as their dream of an independent state died. Without the British troops there to support them, U.S. expansion westward began in earnest.

Below: Signatures and wax seals on the Treaty of Ghent indicate both sides' agreement to its terms. The treaty ended the War of 1812.

GLOSSARY

acquisition The act of taking over ownership of something

allies Nations that are on the same side in a war

ambush To make a surprise attack from a hidden position

artillery Large guns, such as cannons, manned by a crew

assimilation The act of becoming more similar, for example when one culture blends in with another

barrage Rapid and repeated artillery fire

blockade The isolation of an enemy location, such as a harbor, in order to prevent the passage of troops and/or supplies

boarding party Sailors that board an enemy ship to capture it

bombard To attack relentlessly using bombs, shells, or other missiles

border The dividing line between two countries

brig A fast, maneuverable ship with two square-rigged masts

campaign A series of planned military actions intended to achieve a certain goal

casualty A person who is killed or wounded in battle

colony An area that belongs to and is ruled by a faraway country. Great Britain, France, and Spain each had colonies in North America.

confederacy A group of people who come together for a specific purpose

Congress In the United States, two groups of representatives who make laws for the nation—the Senate and the House of Representatives

contraband Illegal or forbidden goods

convoy A group that travels together, often for protection

escarpment A steep slope or long cliff

evacuate To leave

flagship The ship that carries the commander of a fleet

fledgling Something that is new and inexperienced

fleet A group of warships under the command of a single leader

fort A military base

free trade Trade between nations without tariffs or other interference from government

frigate A mid-sized, square-rigged warship used during the 1800s

frontier The furthest edge of land that is settled, beyond which the country is wild

governor-general The king or queen's representative in a country within the British commonwealth

H.M.S. Short for "His or Her Majesty's Ship" (used for naming ships in the British Navy)

hull The deck, sides, and bottom of a boat

impressment The act of seizing someone for service to the government

legislative buildings Government buildings where laws are passed and taxes raised and spent

letter of marque A formal document giving someone the government's permission to seize people and/or goods from an enemy nation

lieutenant governor The head of a province or colony appointed by the governor-general

looting Seizing goods in acts of violence, usually in wartime

magazine The room or building in a fort where explosives are stored

massacre To brutally kill a large number of defenseless people

militia A small army of citizens organized by each state who serve as soldiers in emergencies

morale The confidence and feelings of a group of people at a certain time

national anthem A song of loyalty to one's country

nations A federation of Native people who share culture, traditions, and a political system

negotiations Meetings and discussions between two or more opposing sides with the goal of coming to an agreement

Northwest Territory In the United States, land that was being settled in the 1790s. It included present-day Ohio, Indiana, Illinois, Michigan, Wisconsin, and parts of Minnesota.

outpost A small military camp away from the main army which is used to guard against surprise attack

overrun To invade or occupy

patriotic Loyal to one's country

president The elected head of the U.S. government

privateer Someone licensed to attack enemy ships; the ship belonging to such a person

rampart A wall built to defend an area or fortress

ratified Formally approved by government

regulars Full-time career soldiers

representative Someone who acts or speaks for people, for example as laws are made

retreat To move soldiers away from an enemy

scepter A staff carried by a monarch as a sign of kingship

seaworthy Describes a ship that is safe for voyaging at sea

shipyard A place where ships are built and repaired

siege The blockade of a city or fort until it is forced to surrender

Six Nations The six Iroquois tribes: the Mohawk, Cayuga, Onondaga, Oneida, Seneca, and Tuscarora

surrender To give up and stop fighting

theater A large geographic area where military combat takes place

treaty A formal agreement between two parties, usually to prevent or end a war

U.S.S. Short for "United States Ship" (used for naming ships in the U.S. Navy)

War Hawk One of a group of congressmen from the South and West, who wanted to go to war with Great Britain in 1812

CHRONOLOGY

1783

Treaty of Paris ends the American Revolutionary War

1803

Jefferson's Louisiana Purchase means the United States doubles in size

1811

November 7 Battle of Tippecanoe

1812

June 18 United States declares war against Great Britain

July 12 U.S. General William Hull invades Canada at Sandwich

July 17 The British capture Fort Mackinack

August 15 Fort Dearborn Massacre

August 16 Surrender of Fort Detroit

August 19 U.S.S. *Constitution* captures H.M.S. *Guerriere*

October 13 Battle of Queenston Heights; Sir Isaac Brock is killed

October 18 U.S.S. *Wasp* captures H.M.S. *Frolic*

October 25 U.S.S. *United States* captures H.M.S. *Macedonian*

December 29 U.S.S. *Constitution* sinks H.M.S. *Java*

1813

January 23 River Raisin Massacre

April 27 Battle of York

May 25 Battle of Fort George begins

June 1 H.M.S. *Shannon* captures U.S.S. *Chesapeake*

June 6 Battle of Stoney Creek

June 24 Battle of Beaver Dams

August 30 Fort Mims Massacre

September 10 Battle of Lake Erie

September 26 Harrison retakes Detroit

October 5 Battle of the Thames; Tecumseh is killed

October 26 Battle of the Chateauguay

November 11 Battle of Crysler's Farm

December 18 Recapture of Fort Niagara

1814

March 27 Battle of Horseshoe Bend

July 25 Battle of Lundy's Lane

August 2 Siege of Fort Erie begins

August 4 Battle of Mackinack Island

August 24 Burning of Washington

September 11 Battle of Lake Champlain (also known as the Battle of Plattsburgh)

September 13–14 Bombardment of Fort McHenry

September 26–27 Battle of Fayal

December 15 Hartford Convention begins

December 24 Treaty of Ghent is signed

1815

January 8 Battle of New Orleans

February 11 The British capture Fort Bowyer

February 18 Ratified treaties exchanged; war is officially over

MORE INFORMATION

Books

Berton, Pierre. *Flames Across the Border: 1813–1814*. Toronto: McClelland and Stewart, 1981.

Berton, Pierre. *The Invasion of Canada, 1812-1813*. Toronto: McClelland and Stewart, 1980.

Dale, Ronald J. *The Invasion of Canada: Battles of the War of 1812*. Toronto: J. Lorimer, 2001.

Hitsman, J. Mackay, and Donald E. Graves. *The Incredible War of 1812: A Military History*. Toronto, Ont: Robin Brass Studio, 2002.

Smolinski, Diane, and Henry Smolinski. *Battles of the War of 1812*. Chicago, Ill: Heinemann Library, 2003.

Stefoff, Rebecca. *The War of 1812*. New York: Benchmark Books, 2001.

DVDs

History Channel Presents: The War of 1812 DVD Set. This two-disc collection covers the involvement and achievements of the United States in the war.

War of 1812. This four-part documentary series from the National Film Board of Canada provides a Canadian perspective on the war.

WEBSITES

Archives of Ontario Exhibit: The War of 1812
www.archives.gov.on.ca/english/on-line-exhibits/1812/index.aspx

The Maryland War of 1812 Bicentennial Commission
http://starspangled200.org/Pages/Home.aspx

Naval History and Heritage: War of 1812
www.history.navy.mil/commemorations/1812/1812-index.htm

The Niagara Official War of 1812 Bicentennial
www.visit1812.com/

The Niagara 1812 Legacy Council
www.discover1812.com/

BIBLIOGRAPHY

The following books and websites were used as sources of the primary evidence included in this book:

Berton, Pierre. *Flames Across the Border: 1813–1814*. Toronto: McClelland and Stewart, 1981.

Berton, Pierre. *The Invasion of Canada, 1812–1813*. Toronto: McClelland and Stewart, 1980.

Bosco, Peter I. *The War of 1812*. Brookfield, Conn: Millbrook Press, 1991.

Conlin, Joseph R. *The American Past: A Survey of American History*. Cengage Learning, 2009.

Crump, Jennifer. *The War of 1812: Heroes of a Great Canadian Victory*. Altitude Publishing Canada Ltd., 2007.

Dale, Ronald J. *The Invasion of Canada: Battles of the War of 1812*. Toronto: J. Lorimer, 2001.

Graves, Donald E. *Field of Glory: The Battle of Crysler's Farm, 1813*. Toronto, Ont: Robin Brass Studio, 1999.

Hitsman, J. Mackay, and Donald E. Graves. *The Incredible War of 1812: A Military History*. Toronto, Ont: Robin Brass Studio, 2002.

Malcomson, Robert. *A Very Brilliant Affair: The Battle of Queenston Heights, 1812.* Annapolis, Md: Naval Institute Press, 2003.

Malcomson, Robert. *Lords of the Lake: The Naval War on Lake Ontario, 1812–1814.* Annapolis, Md: Naval Institute Press, 1998.

Smolinski, Diane, and Henry Smolinski. *Battles of the War of 1812*. Chicago, Ill: Heinemann Library, 2003.

Stefoff, Rebecca. *The War of 1812*. New York: Benchmark Books, 2001.

Historical Narratives of Early Canada: http://www.uppercanadahistory.ca/brock/brock4.html
Naval History and Heritage Command:
    http://www.history.navy.mil/trivia/trivia02.htm
    http://www.history.navy.mil/bios/hull_isaac.htm
    http://www.history.navy.mil/library/online/burning_washington.htm
Rediscover 1812 website: http://rediscover1812.com/
The Archives of Ontario: http://www.archives.gov.on.ca/english/on-line-exhibits/1812/1812/index.aspx
The Smithsonian: http://americanhistory.si.edu/starspangledbanner/
The White House website: http://www.whitehouse.gov/about/presidents/

INDEX